JOURNEYS

Towards Brighton

JOURNEYS

Train Journeys through British Landscapes

Francia Turner

DAVID & CHARLES
Newton Abbot   London

To the memory of my mother,
and to Dr Pamela MacKinnon,
a scientist with an artist's eye

British Library Cataloguing in Publication Data

Turner, Francia
  Journeys: train journeys through British
  landscapes
  1. Great Britain. Journeys by buses
  I. Title
  914.1'04858

ISBN 0-7153-9322-7

Printed in Hong Kong
for David & Charles Publishers plc
Brunel House Newton Abbot Devon

Contents

Scotland

The Midlands to Hereford

Acknowledgements

Throughout the making of this book there have been many people involved with its development. My appreciation goes to all of the following:

William G. Richards, Head of Commercial Publishing of the English Tourist Board, who gave me invaluable advice throughout the production of this book; Richard Dorsett, Commercial Publishing Consultant to the ETB, whose practical suggestions and belief in the project were of great help; Alistair Hankey, Director of Information Services of the ETB, for his support of the project.

Mike Bowler of British Rail, who supported the proposal from our first meeting and during the long development period to publication.

Also at the ETB: Michael Dewing, the Publishing Control Manager, for his interest and advice; Tessa Williams, for reading the text and assiduously crossing my Ts, dotting my Is and putting in my hyphens; Julia Froggatt and Susie Thompson, for their assistance and interest in the book's progress. Sheila Martin, Manager of the British Travel Centre in London, provided valuable help in its promotion.

St Hilda's College, Oxford, for accepting me as their first art student.

Pauline Stainer, for her involvement in the early stages of preparation; Penny McEwan, for her contribution.

Michael De Luca, Editorial Director of David & Charles Publishers, for his enthusiasm and encouragement; Faith Glasgow, the Art Editor, whose insight and sensitivity to my work was very important and with whom I enjoyed working; Mike Lyons for a thoughtful and well-designed cover, and Brian Holmes, for his enthusiastic approach and creative marketing.

Studio Edmark, Oxford: Jeremy Moeran and Jean Hunt for their care in the photography of the original artwork.

My father and my children, Riga and Dylan, who have consistently given me their love, support and understanding.

And finally, the staff of British Rail, who were always interested and helpful during the hundreds of hours I spent working on the railway.

Introduction

When I made my first drawing from the train six years ago, I never imagined what adventures and discoveries lay ahead. Motivated by my feelings for the British countryside, I embarked on a journey which would take me travelling back and forth throughout Britain, developing a relationship with the island, from the northernmost tip of Scotland to the furthest point west in Cornwall, from Welsh coastal plains to the flat fenlands of East Anglia.

It started with an unusual combination of events. In 1981 I had begun studying full-time at art school. Having worked for many years on my own, I wanted to make the most of my time there. In the first year I often spent over twenty hours each week drawing from the figure, working on poses set from thirty seconds up to three hours. During the quick poses I had to learn how to look for the essence in the structure of the figure and convey it in the shortest amount of time. Anatomy classes helped by giving a greater understanding of the underlying form.

A surprising progression over the next year was to find myself using the skills of quick observation gained in the life drawing classes and applying them to the landscape, from within the perfect vehicle: one in which a studio was provided, with a comfortable seat, a table, and large windows giving panoramic views and a constantly moving and stimulating scene to draw.

For years before beginning this book, I had, on every rail journey, imagined what it would be like to pull the emergency cord and stop the train in order to draw a scene from the carriage window. Reason however, prevailed, for no matter how spectacular the view, a £50.00 fine was too high a price to pay for such a brief artistic moment. But thoughts of the scenery offered by rail travel remained and formed a great part of my appreciation of the British countryside.

For my birthday in January 1983, my son gave me an unruled A4 notebook and six pencils with a range of hard and soft leads. I was eager to experiment using these materials to draw the landscape while the train was in motion, and began working tentatively on my trips to London during term vacations. Soon the notebook was filled and I had progressed to an A3 drawing pad using pastels, charcoal and conte crayon which could capture the immediacy of the movement and cover large areas quickly. I started by making an outline of the anatomy of the landscape, which would then be filled in on each successive journey. Something that had been previously missed would be added. Each picture was worked on in that way until it was finished.

Having used bright colours in most of my earlier work, making monochrome pictures using black, white and greys was a new departure. I wanted to make the shades of black and white become or seem like other colours to the eye. After working only in monochrome for over a year, the time seemed right to introduce the more complex process of colour. When drawing in monochrome the structure of the picture was the most important element – bringing in colour meant having to observe not only form but an enormous variety of everchanging tones. This transition took until early in 1986.

Another influence on the book was a growing interest in anthropology and archaeology. After graduating from art school in 1984 I started attending lectures at the Pitt Rivers Museum, Oxford. The course in prehistoric archaeology showed me a new way of looking at land forms, recognising hill fortresses, burial mounds and ancient plough lines which have all left their mark and been assimilated into our present-day countryside. I began to see from another perspective the history of shapes and forms – Man's influence on the surface patterns, size of fields and forests.

By the summer of 1986 various exhibitions of the drawings had been held. I was encouraged to approach British Rail with the idea of making a book based upon these pictures; in October of that year I spoke to British Rail, who suggested that the English Tourist Board might also be interested. The idea was enthusiastically accepted by both organizations, who agreed to endorse the project. British Rail assisted me in my travels and the English Tourist Board was very supportive during every stage of the book's development. As work progressed, the keen interest and endorsement of the Wales Tourist Board and the Scottish Tourist Board was also received.

Now, travelling throughout Britain, I was able to see the island as a whole. Each new journey added to my enthusiasm. It was an incredible challenge, which became even greater when, after completing a number of pieces, it was agreed that specific landmarks would complement the more general landscapes. The composite pictures allowed me the freedom of putting together the moving jigsaw of trees, hills, rivers, fields or mountains that quickly passed by. The recognised landmarks, on the other hand, took much longer and continually tested my observational skills.

I began work on these in the West Country with Dawlish, The Ness and St Ives, which took between fifteen and twenty trips each. The buildings came later and were the most difficult: Harlech, Criccieth and Conwy castles each took up to thirty journeys to complete. They, along with the rest of the work in progress, were kept in a portfolio which I carried with me on every journey. No picture was ever worked on after I left the train – some remained in the portfolio for weeks until they were finished. Criss-crossing between towns, cities and countries and juggling timetables in an attempt to get as much as possible accomplished in one day was an extraordinary experience. More often than not I barely managed to catch my connecting train. Short winter days meant only being able to draw until mid-afternoon, while finding sufficient space to work during peak hours also posed problems.

The magnificent Welsh castle of Harlech presented its own particular difficulties. On the north-west Wales coast, there is a single track line from Barmouth to Pwllheli with a changeover station at Harlech. Here the single track divides into two, making it possible for trains to pass at this point. A token must be handed from one train to the other, allowing each train to proceed on its journey.

In order to get a view of Harlech Castle from the north, I would go to Pwllheli. I had to start drawing immediately upon entering the train as the castle can only be seen for about a minute after leaving the station.

On the return trip, having also worked on the Criccieth Castle picture and

the view to Mount Snowdon near Porthmadog, I would brace myself to draw as much of Harlech as possible before literally throwing all of my materials together and descending from the train. I then had to race up the steps of the railway bridge, anorak flying, in an attempt to board the northbound carriage before the token had been exchanged. This was done several times in a day until the picture was finished.

I had not planned to write the book as well as making the pictures. It was originally to have been an anthology, but as the work developed, the English Tourist Board felt that it would be enhanced by words written at the same time as the pictures.

I was encouraged to use the reflections I had been writing since my initial trip to Scotland in December 1986. The spectacular mountain views had so moved me that I began writing on small pieces of paper, as I had not brought a notebook with me. I even wrote on sheets of my A2 drawing pad using charcoal drawings sticks. Eventually there were forty-six filled notebooks which needed editing and compiling – a task which took much longer than I had anticipated.

Now that the book is complete, drawings from the train will continue to form a major part of my work. Each time I board a train I am inspired by seeing the changes that take place in the land, almost as if overnight. The dark and light contrasts of ploughed fields and ripe grain, the strength and delicacy of trees and wild shrubs or the drama of clouds preparing for an imminent storm all form part of a sweeping overview, a continuous moving picture that passes before our eyes.

From the cone-shaped mountains in the far north of Scotland approaching Thurso and Wick, to the turquoise waters of St Ives, on the north west tip of Cornwall; from the Welsh valleys, headlands and mountains made of slate, to the red-rust coastal cliffs of south Devon; from Whitby in north-east Yorkshire to the white limestone cliffs of the Kent Coast: it is an extraordinary mixture, a composite landscape rich with striking variation.

On every journey I wonder what colours and forms will be presented to me and in what new way I will be able to portray them.

F.T.
September 1988

FENS, ELY TO KING'S LYNN

After Cambridge,
flat fenlands begin.
Reclaimed from marshes,
with deep black soil,
a contrast to tiny green seedlings
in perfect rows, and straw lines
juxtaposed against brilliant yellow
rapeseed fields.
To Ely
and its remarkable cathedral.
Tarpaulin-covered river boats
near flooded marshland homes of
swans and water fowl, to Littleport
and continuous windswept fields.
Scarecrows, jackets flying,
attempt to fend off persistent gulls.
A windmill in the distance and
changes in the hue of the land,
warmed by red earth minerals,
to Downham Market.
Horses grazing, pinto and dappled,
and semicircular bridges above narrow
reed-lined canals to Magdalen Road.
Blossomed orchards act as
windbreaks approaching King's Lynn.

East Anglia

CHAPEL OF THE HOLY GHOST, BASINGSTOKE

From the train heading south
at Basingstoke can be seen
majestic archways, cloisters
of the sixteenth-century
Chapel of the Holy Ghost,
laid to ruin
during the time of Cromwell.
Edges crumbling,
asymmetrical.
Creepers growing through
sand-coloured cornices.
Powerfully built,
with delicate, chiselled forms
on weathered brick.
Striking, against
the cemetery background
it dominates.

NEW FOREST

Dorset's south coast,
Poole and Bournemouth,
through Hampshire's New Forest.
Ponies seen near marsh patches,
leading to land with new growth
of conifers.
Occasional villages, found
amidst thick woodlands, stretching
between vast, open plains.
Broad, distant landscape.
Bracken, scrub, windswept heathland
and young plantations of oak and beech,
spreading northward.

SOUTHAMPTON HARBOUR

North through the New Forest,
suddenly from a different landscape,
technically created,
emerges Southampton harbour.
Flowering cherries, terraces,
towards the dockyards.
Gas towers, warehouses,
containers in rows, lined by the
parallel road's daffodils.
Ocean-going machinery for
world's shipping and freight.
Giant cranes, moving and removing,
preparing for export and import,
despatching and receiving goods;
and docked in the harbour waters, ships.
Freighters, tankers, tugs,
sailing boats and dinghies,
awaiting passage.

TOWARDS DOVER

Passing London's impressive skyline,
with office blocks and brick terraces,
copper spire churches,
parks and marigold gardens,
cricket and bowls, to Bromley South.
Through mill towns with chimney stacks
dominating the landscape,
thick copses, tree formations.
Past chalk hills bordering
the River Medway
and ancient Rochester Castle
overlooking the estuary.
To Chatham, Medway town,
with horses in pastures
down to docklands.
Through Gillingham Tunnel,
Rainham Maltings and allotments
to Newington and Sittingbourne

with black and white farmhouses
and tree-hedged orchards,
the 'Garden of England', to Faversham.
Fertile, cultivated country
where yellow roses
climb over railway fences
approaching Canterbury.
Past its cathedral and
old stone and flint churches,
to grazing-lands and hops
in even, posted rows.
Oast-house farms nearing the sea
towards Dover Priory,
with views of Dover Castle
overseeing city and surrounding land.
Exposed chalk, and sea winds
ruffling trees to Dover Western Dock.

DOVER

Cliffs, not only white
limestone chalk,
from Folkestone to Dover Priory.
Fissures, space for growth
of plants nourished by sea winds,
forming lacy, jagged patterns
on crusty stone.
The cliff forms, constantly changing
relief sculptures.
Salt-eroded, wind-removed,
powerful entrance to
England's south-eastern coast.

ELY TO IPSWICH

Ely, south-east through flat
racing country with groves
of thick pines.
The train runs high, towering over
sweeping trees and fertile
mid-Suffolk landscape to
Bury St Edmunds.
Beautifully made station,
wrought iron painted white
against shadowed dark-red brick.
Land, gentle slopes, darkly ploughed.
Rabbits and pheasants feed in fields
near the track to Stowmarket,
passing vast factories
of yellow-white timber
to Ipswich.

East Anglia

NORFOLK BROADS

From Lowestoft's thriving port
to Oulton Broad North,
past moored yachts and river cruisers.
The Broads spread northward into
the Norfolk landscape.
In the distance,
orange, white and ultramarine sails
appear to be travelling on land
under reed hedges,
until the train approaches the winding
waterways near Somerleyton.
Dark rust-tipped reeds line the water
to Haddiscoe, passing windmills
and vast stretches of flat
cattle country, open plains with
tufts of wild grasses,
to Reedham's river crossing.
Views for miles to Cantley and
an expansive sky that spreads over
flat marshland thick with vegetation,
secure home for Broadland birds
and wildlife.
To Brundall, boatyard and lush land
following the River Wensum's
flowering banks
to Norwich.

East Anglia

NORWICH TO COLCHESTER

Land surrounding Norwich,
warm red-ochre earth,
straight with sharp edges
and black and white thatched houses,
to Diss.
Ground shimmering green and
polished brown,
to Stowmarket past wild and cultivated flowers,
fields and allotments.

To Ipswich,
large flourishing port.
Containers and cranes,
large dock buildings leading to
rounded farmland and orchards.
Yachts anchored in the harbour
at Manningtree, where
the estuary fills with black, white
and rust sea birds.
Gulls settle in large
evenly ploughed fields,
soft rows moving upwards,
planted in zig-zag patterns.
Fertile, light cocoa-coloured earth,
tinged with pink,
to Colchester.

East Anglia

ERSK VALLEY

From Ipswich port,
the Ersk valley
veers to the right
of the Norwich line,
to Westerfield.
Forests of newly planted trees
and soft rolling farmland
with serpentine streams running through.
Tributaries of the River Deben
with banks becoming havens
for boats assembled
at the lowering tide.
Farmland turns to sea marshes:
dry-docked yachts await summer
and some are water-moored
by the harbour at Woodbridge,
with its painted cream timber
tide mill.
Open water to Melton
with descending sea-birds
over river-swept paddocks
and farms to Wickham Market.
Cottages of Suffolk pink,
flint churches and
mill-shaped barns.
Past fields of ripe wheat
and barley to Saxmundham
and Lowestoft.

East Anglia

WESTBURY TO TAUNTON

Land changing near Westbury,
still red brick
and hilly dark ground,
geometric hedgerows,
brown, richest black earth.
Not soft or sunburnt colours,
but deep contrasts.
Black and white cattle
stand up and out
as if cut cardboard,
approaching
Westbury's famous landmark.
The White Horse,
with its sand-dune
corrugated, companion hills.
Ripple hills, reaching out
to peak above the magic horse,
not the Ancient
but the Modern,
sculpted
in chalky Berkshire, Wiltshire stone.
Gulls practise aerodynamics above
newly sown fields.
Cattle graze in their allotted enclosures.
And the view, shimmering, moving light.
Houses in clusters
becoming stone from brick.
Afternoon sun rays
bathe the close hills
and sun pockets attract
brilliant responses
from the flat farmland.

West Country

TAUNTON, EXETER, DAWLISH

Taunton, changing for Bridgwater,
heading west,
the pace changes.
Cathedrals and kitchen gardens,
freight depot, coal cars and carriages.
Thickly trimmed hedgerows,
sheep keeping grass to a minimum,
hay in black plastic stacks.
Hills forming near Exeter,
warm, even red earth
beginning to alter the scene.
Autumn colours, hot rusts, bright death
of summer leaves;
grass still brilliant green
but trees betray their summer fullness.
Leaves are scattered –
some hold on
but imminent winds
will mean their flight.

Exeter, mouth of the River Exe,
sunshine on the out tide,
shellfishermen and
sun patterns on flat mud
through to Dawlish.
Many boats are
not yet moored for winter.
Mid-October,
twice as many boats as May,
all hoping for the warmth to remain.

West Country

RAIN ON WINDOW –
LISKEARD

Nearing St Austell,
from Liskeard,
rain smudges,
criss-cross,
darts across,
propelled in lined tracks
on glazed panes.
Causing blurred visions
of a land
whose structure,
like a prism,
is broken down,
but not disconnected.

West Country

ST IVES

St Ives,
turquoise waters, palms,
ultra sun-rays
glow through curled kelp,
bringing Mediterranean light.
Rock formations, stunning,
sharp, jagged granite,
wide sculptures holding up
the West of England.

Across the bay,
a lighthouse perches
on its uneven rock base,
an island in the sound.
Land masses, retreating,
famous backdrop of Cornwall's
northern coast,
outlined behind and beyond.

Orange buoys stand out
as the sea's constant movement
opens its route
to the changing currents.

Autumn sandcastles,
melted by the waves,
are seen as the train
follows curves
along the coast to Carbis Bay.
Cliff houses watch the breaking surf
on vast, open, yellow tan beaches.
Wild dune grass and smooth golf courses,
cross through to boats, sandmoored below Lelant,
where waters have subsided,
exposing seaweed forests and marbled
jigsaw mudflats to St Erth.

West Country

DAWLISH TO TEIGNMOUTH

Exeter to Dawlish,
cliffs, striking coloured walls
against the sea.
'Parson and Clerk' rocks.
Clerk in the sea,
Parson on the Mount.
Rich, stratified stone,
red, thick rust,
warm, crumbling, soft.
Distant orange on horizon line.
Close, enclosed,
Parson and Clerk Tunnel within,
then bright, clear without.
Clarity of light on waves,
wind pronouncing, provoking foam
against the track.
Teignmouth, with sea-front terraces and
Red heart name sign, guarding the coast.

West Country

TIN MINE, REDRUTH

St Erth, looking through
to the sea,
to Hayle and small towns,
blending together
on the peninsula run.
Grass-covered dunes
and compressed trees,
coated with salt film spray
exposed to constant gusts
over flat expanses,
to Camborne.

Tin on the landscape.
Scattered mines
remaining, to Redruth.
Empty mine ruins,
windows, stacks.
Buildings, non-operative,
broken stone,
sculptured shells
of windblown,
rain-stained walls.
Ivy vines, clothing
the manmade remnants
of a mining past.

THE NESS, SHALDON

Towards Newton Abbot,
across from Teignmouth,
Shaldon, the patchwork town
with bridge attracting,
inviting, across to red
earth-made, man-made,
safe harbour and
leading to stratified cliff
on the Channel's edge,
the Ness Headland.
Like a quilted country
of threaded hedgerows
and silken straw.

West Country

ST MICHAEL'S MOUNT

St Erth to Penzance,
ocean farmland and
flights of sea birds
over deep-tide mudbanks.
Rows of pebble boulders.
Coastal sightings, from Marazion.
The sea and granite castle
rising from the sea.
St Michael's Mount,
island monastery, fortress,
blending with the rock,
severed from the land,
at high-tide
standing alone.

West Country

PLYMOUTH TO BODMIN PARKWAY

Exhilarating crossing,
Plymouth to Saltash, Devon to Cornwall.
The River Tamar, dividing-line
across an impressive harbour scene.
Past red sandstone castle
to a circular boatyard on high ground,
above a winding river tributary.
Cottages dotted amongst tall trees
and hill farmland at St Germans.
Newly planted fields
alongside thickly filled pastures,
streams and fertile, lush land,
overlapping grass hills.
Strong hedgerow fences, no need for stone.
Sheep in the healthy landscape.

Nearing Liskeard,
the white and pastel-coloured town
in the specialized Cornish line,
the sea is felt but unseen.
The trees are sea-swept, sea trees.
The sea exists, probably over the closest hill.
Then, taking us by surprise,
the thick, deep forests
approaching Bodmin Parkway come into view.
Fir trees, on rounded, touchable hills
with stream flowing by the track.
A forest oasis
in a rich green desert of farmland.

West Country

CONWY CASTLE

From Chester along the sea edge,
Welsh towns and villages in mid-winter
alternate with flooded fields,
white with sea birds.
Mountains nearing breaking waves
past Rhyl to Llandudno Junction,
with views of thirteenth-century
Conwy Castle.
Eight powerful rounded towers
across the River Conwy, enclosed in
their walled town, protect the
North Wales coast.
Deganwy and the Victorian terraced
Llandudno, through to
the island of Anglesey.

SHREWSBURY TOWARDS LLANDEILO

Shrewsbury and Knighton,
south through central Wales valleys.
Past Sugar Loaf mountain's
pine forests
and panoramic views
from Cynghordy viaduct,
to Llandovery.
Then broad cultivated land
with cattle and sheep
dotted in mist-dampened pastures.
At a distance, backdrops,
cone-shaped pointed mountains,
tinted peaks, russet-orange
with moss patches,
to Llandeilo.

Wales

PORTHMADOG –
VIEWS TO SNOWDON

South from Criccieth,
passing steep cliffs
with vertically lined
rock faces,
approaching Porthmadog.
From the train, striking views
to Mount Snowdon
and its powerful companion peaks.
Lands combining highest
Welsh mountains and
proximity to the sea,
with soft, sloping moorland
leading to the fern-lined track.

Wales

THE VALLEYS

From Cardiff,
starting point of the Valley lines,
Rhondda and Merthyr.
Past Llandaff and turreted
cliffside Castle Coch,
to Pontypridd, where the track divides.
Following the Merthyr line,
high fir forests with towns
nestling below to Quakers' Yard.
The gradient steepens,
with trees well-defined
on the crests of hills,
as the train moves upwards
through fern-lined slopes
and conifer plantations.
To Merthyr Vale,
past rows of neatly terraced gardens
and views to distant peaks,
the Brecon Beacons.
Passing high valley farms
to Merthyr Tydfil.

Wales

HARLECH CASTLE

Barmouth to Pensarn,
white Welsh cottages and
sea-blown farms enclosed by
lichen-covered dry stone walls.
Sheep wander between enclosures
to Llandanwg,
then narrow strip of land
just wide enough for the train to pass.
To Harlech,
giant square fortress,
dominating the dunes,
commanding the sea.
A structure whose size and strength
would protect
and keep at bay assailants.
From within its castle deep stone walls,
views to Pwllheli, the Llŷn peninsula
and the Snowdonia range.

Wales

TOWARDS PEMBROKE

Llanelli and open beach coast
to Pembrey and Burry Port,
with farms that have
the feel of the sea.
To Carmarthen and Whitland,
thick valley green
highlighted by mauve, yellow
and white wild flowers.
Open flat lands
leading to cultivated slopes.
Changing landscape
across broad valleys and
south-west Wales farms
with views to a hundred miles
and beyond.
Square stone church towers,
pine hills and
misty high grasses.
Ruled hedges formed by set squares,
sheer lines making straight patterns
leading south to Tenby,
Pembroke and the Bristol Channel.

Wales

BLAENAU FFESTINIOG

Llandudno Junction,
single track,
through vast slate mountains
to Blaenau Ffestiniog.
Quarries, man- and nature-made,
black, grey-violet, reflective.
Sharp-edged pieces of the jigsaw
piled high.
Working remnants.
Mountains whose precious stone
can be chipped
and sliced from the surface,
layer upon layer,
cascading like white water
in the valleys below.

Wales

WELSH BORDERS

Hereford to Abergavenny,
Pontypool and Newport,
just inside and outside
the border.
On the verge,
see-sawing,
teeter-tottering.
Close-cropped trees
uniting and separating
the two countries.
Clouds perch on high branches.
Farms advance and retreat
from the track.
For moments, woodlands
in autumn multi-coloured rows
overtake the view
until the landscape opens again
to Welsh farmland
stretched on a horizontal canvas.

Wales

62

CRICCIETH CASTLE

From Pwllheli, stone town's
wide estuary harbour
where winter sea birds
find shelter.
Through moorland farms
to Criccieth,
with its castle
above the sea
and aware of any dangers
from the land.
Criccieth, early Welsh stronghold,
with two forceful entrance towers
leading to weathered walls.
At the centre of the Llŷn peninsula
watching over Cardigan Bay,
high on its island-like headlands
defending the town below.

Wales

DOLWYDDELAN CASTLE

Through the Conwy valley's
steep forests,
from Llandudno Junction,
to Betws-y-coed,
town of striking dark stone
and white water.
Rugged, fertile country.
Spruce plantations
create deep textures.
Rising peaks protect valley streams
and tiny waterfalls
make their way
down ridged crevices.
To ruins, Dolwyddelan Castle,
twelfth-century stone,
surrounded by terraced mountains,
aged in its open space,
remaining walls
standing against the elements.
Through lace ferns and foliage
in sun-sheltered valleys
to Blaenau Ffestiniog.

Wales

SHEFFIELD TO MANCHESTER

Industrial landscape –
factories and electric pylons
with steel cranes and
water towers.
Cornices on Sheffield station platform,
wooden-slatted and patterned
like nineteenth-century
wrought-iron balconies.
Old yellow brick,
mill buildings
and corrugated warehouses,
built-up landscape of buildings,
some in use,
others functional though
not functioning.
Cracks appear, allowing
green leafy growth.
Farms mingle with industry past Crewe,
co-existing, alternating,
manufacturing, producing,
transporting on
the trade routes of Britain
to Manchester and Liverpool.

TO RAVENGLASS

From Barrow-in-Furness,
mountains and Cumbrian coastal downs.
The landscape becomes wilder
facing the coast.
Handthrown clay hills, pinnacle hills,
open to the elements.
Reeds, marshes, leading to
extraordinary views from Askam
and Kirkby-in-Furness,
where the train appears to enter
straight into rounded peaks.
Through Green Road and Millom,
to Silecroft.
Thickset clouds over
yellow straw mountains,
radiating with olive green
and red-tinged hill cultivation,
to Bootle.
Mustard yellow hills.
A mountain chain of startling colour,
Moss-gold with black between,
To Ravenglass and the sea.

ROSEBERRY TOPPING, NORTH YORKSHIRE

Leaving Whitby,
from Battersby to Gypsy Lane,
the remarkable peak
of Roseberry Topping can be seen.
Standing like a pyramid
and overseeing the
surrounding countryside,
this cone-shaped mound
in a land of gently curving hills
stands out as a challenge
to be reached.
Nearing the summit, bare earth patches
are found on its grass cover,
scarred by the feet of walkers
who attempt its heights.

DARLINGTON –
CORAL STREAK

York to Darlington.
Views to the horizon's edge,
no end in sight.
Sheep easily graze.
Occasional trees and hedge bushes
give texture to the level landscape.
Sun rays through blue-grey storm clouds
colour the flat fields in light,
giving the illusion of silver-green
beneath steel.
Coral streaks glimmer, surprising,
as sun sparks pass through deep clouds
for an instant.

The North

WHITBY ABBEY

From Middlesbrough,
on the Esk Valley line
through villages to Sleights,
with summer growth aligning
and adjusting to the single track.
Moss-covered fences on railway platforms,
past stone cottages to Ruswarp
and high red-brick viaduct.
To Whitby,
where the River Esk flows through
to the North Sea.
Fishing boats fill the harbour
beneath Whitby's thirteenth-century abbey,
standing one hundred and ninety-nine
steps above the town,
seen for miles from bright
gorse-covered moorland.
Powerful stone-built remnants,
imposing frame, empty arches
of the remaining creviced walls.
Striking sandstone forms
above the cliff's edge.

SKIPTON TO CARLISLE

Skipton, unmortared stone walls,
with stream by the track.
Exquisite, rounded hills,
deep rich green, cultivated high.
Panoramic Yorkshire views.
The Dales, spectacular land-forms,
in tinted layers of green.
To Settle, nestled amongst hills
of farmland.
Grey-stone town,
rising on a slope, with wide rock faces.
Stone fences on the crests of hills,
protecting, enclosing sheep and cottages.
Reaching stratified quarries,
to Horton in Ribblesdale,
Yorkshire Dales National Park.
The land, sanded and watered down,
not jagged but filed by the elements.
Clouds settle in tiny valleys
between each semi-circular hill.
To Ribblehead, through two-mile-long
Blenmire tunnel.
Pine forests climbing higher,
with farmland in steep valleys,
tunnels following tunnels.
Yorkshire Dales, simplicity of patterns
well defined, with sweeping slopes
like waves approaching moss-covered hills,
leading to the Cumbrian city
of Carlisle.

The North

78

STAFFORD TO PRESTON

North from Stafford,
farms on higher ground,
grazing lands
rising from the track.
Sheep and Friesian cattle
share elevated pastures.
Wooden bridges cross over
tiny canals,
with fields leading up hill slopes.
Trees becoming horizontal planes,
on vertical, layered farmland,
unruled but even, forms in motion,
to Crewe.
Flat valleys extend northwards
to Warrington Bank Quay,
and towns and villages
come together, merging, spreading
towards distant, haze-covered hills
to Preston.

The North

CREWE TOWARDS CARLISLE

Land becoming steeper
approaching the Lake District.
Deep leaf-green fields
and close-cropped borders
to Lancaster.
Hills, with vertical cliffs,
deeply forested.
Hedges, dry stone and bush
to Oxenholme.
Hill farmland, curved distant
undulating shapes,
forms on a painted landscape.
Lake District watercolour,
spreading, unfolding.
Yellow-tinged mountains,
sand-coloured peaks
with tawny green ridges.
English highlands, uplands,
glowing stone and sheep pastures
spreading to Carlisle.

CROOKED SPIRE, CHESTERFIELD

Between Derby and Sheffield,
Chesterfield comes into view,
with its twisted
contorted landmark.
A spire
beguiling the eye,
defying the laws
of structural engineering.
One of England's wonders,
riveting our attention
as we pass from close
Derbyshire hills,
through a town inspired by
its Leaning Tower of the North.

The North

KINGUSSIE

Kingussie, clear late January,
clusters of dark forest trees
against slate-coloured hills.
Moss, grass with small ice-flooded patches
remain from the last storm.
Coal piled high for solid-fuel heating
alongside Newtonmore station,
and the occasional winter beige sheep.
Colour mint-green and straw
showing through snow-brushed pines.
Great covered mountains
becoming bare slopes.
Isolated farm on golden hillside
between fir and maroon buds.

McCAIG'S TOWER, OBAN

From Glasgow past Tainault,
succeeding peaks frame the stillest of waters
to Connel ferry,
and the land's edge follows
a winding pathway around
Loch Etive.
Mountain sheep graze
on rugged, heather-covered slopes,
towards the highland fishing port
of Oban.
Views from the harbour
lead up past large
Victorian sandstone houses
to McCaig's Tower,
unfinished monument
of heavy granite,
standing above the town.
A Roman coliseum on a Scottish hillside.

Scotland

TOWARDS
KYLE OF LOCHALSH

Towards Kyle of Lochalsh,
Achnasheen to Strathcarron.
Sun brings brilliant orange to
the rusty bracken.
Shadows on the loch.
Reflections of golds, maroons
and deep forest greens,
with giant blue-horse clouds
over mountains.
The train moves slowly
around the edge of the loch.
A solitary white croft
on the opposite shore,
like a topsy-turvy castle
shimmering the waters at Stromeferry,
with little islands rising out.
Glimpses of snow-covered mountains
through hazy clouds.
Across the bay,
a red and white lighthouse;
and through an open land of rocks
then islands and inlets,
pink and peach-coloured buds
soften the lichen-covered stones.

Scotland

RANNOCH

Riding parallel to mountain ridges,
into deep frost-filled valleys,
north from Crianlarich.
Dove-grey gulls tipped in white
hover over Bridge of Orchy.
Land descending,
trees on the incline
past streams to Rannoch Moor.
Moon landscapes of ancient peat,
wild and spare, with firs, conifers,
separate and in groves,
and glacial stones scattered
as if thrown by hand
from another age.
To Rannoch and Corrour.
Peaks made of prisms,
with sharp, angular edges.
Track runs alongside vertical cliffs,
above frozen valleys
to Tulloch.
Passing cloud-covered summits
and loch reflecting forests of pine,
fully grown,
towards Fort William.

Scotland

BORDERS, NEAR BERWICK

From Berwick-upon-Tweed,
England's northernmost town.
Three miles to the border,
with cliffs above the North Sea.
Entering Scotland,
a red stone castle
stands out on the landscape.
Gold and green farmlands
lie on the earth's ribcage
like a blanket,
covering undulating rocky mounds.
Sea-blown trees
and wild pink blossoms
combine with white clipped sheep.
Deep green fir plantations,
inner and outer sea cliffs,
water views interspersed with rows
of evenly planted crops.

The track runs parallel to the road
and glimpses of the sea are broken
by powered industry and lighthouse, alone.
Modern factories appear between farms.
Wild flowers and shrubs take precedence
until arriving at Dunbar Station,
where fuchsias and tulips fill
the landscaped garden platform,
backdrop for Victorian hotels.
Enormous rock island in the bay at Dunbar
captures the eye, with cone-shaped
mountain in coastal distance.
Scottish stone towns and villages,
some red sandstone, some grey,
make their way towards the outskirts of Edinburgh,
where wild red poppies have overtaken
vacant land.

Scotland

94

AVIEMORE –
DRUMMAKER PASS

Inverness to Aviemore,
to Kingussie through Drummaker Pass.
Winter white heights
through narrow passes from Inverness,
arriving at Aviemore station.
Craggy peaks feel never-ending,
in stark rows, rolling back
as if marching on the landscape.
The stone has been
juggled, jumbled.
Fierce movement over millions of years
has formed giants,
heavy-footed, moving masses,
heading south.
They approach us
on our voyaging, winding line,
and as quickly, step back,
allowing us to stare
at their strength.

Scotland

NEAR PITLOCHRY

From Blair Atholl,
down darkly clad mountains,
soft rusts and maroons.
Track follows the river around
past closely aligned trees.
The train moves slowly through a narrow pass,
steep escarpment, to Pitlochry.
Land glowing with highland colours.
Streams forming tiny waterfalls
scurry down hillsides.
Tree-filled slopes,
russet and dark green
to Pitlochry station,
with its painted fountain of
white, red, green and gold.
The stone-preserved town,
spreading up a gentle slope.

Leading to Dunkeld and Perth.
Rolling farmland with mountains
in the distance,
ice still lies on hard earth,
frozen snow lakes.
Sheep break through patchy frost, for grass.

Scotland

GEORGEMAS JUNCTION

Lands at the top of Scotland,
Thurso and Wick.
Cone-shaped hills,
pyramids.
Empty yet full,
barren yet fertile,
spacious, wild, wide
to Georgemas Junction,
Scotscalder and Altnabreac,
Caithness county.
A landscape from another land.
Icy deserts,
frozen dunes.
Windswept,
open to the changing clouds,
heavy, perching on triangular
mountains.

Then, through a winding route
of heather-encrusted hills,
sloping farmland,
castles and sea views,
to Inverness.

Scotland

KILCHURN CASTLE

From Oban and Taynuilt,
past mountains formed
as if by sculpted construction
draped with moss-green velvet.
The River Orchy widens towards
the entrance to Loch Awe
at Falls of Cruachan.
The loch opens to its full depth
and space, with tree-covered islands
emerging.
Fir trees reach the water's edge,
then, in a stage setting
of enormous peaks surrounding the
mountain loch, Kilchurn Castle appears
on a peninsula jutting into reflective waters.
Multi-levelled, with round towers,
stone, weathered, cracked;
worn by centuries' rains
and mists.
Force of the ancient stronghold,
home and fortress;
Scottish strength in a landscape
of extreme beauty.
A solitary edifice, refuge.

Scotland

STIRLING TO DUNDEE

Stirling and Dunblane,
mid-summer.
Fast river rapids, wide canals
through rolling country
of broad pastures and
fir trees, thickly planted.
Layered hills covered
in light violet heather,
yellow and cream wild flowers
mix with thistles, reeds and dry bracken,
to Gleneagles.
Peaks becoming steeper
and land opening out
onto a spectacular panorama
of straight-edged farms
in deep blue-green, straw
and chestnut brown.
Hay stacked in round bales
on large close-cut fields
to Perth.
Mountains now becoming
creviced rock-faces.
A tiny castle-fortress
watches over the land
from high on a craggy ridge.
Dark olive conifers stand out
against cultivated, bright green hillsides.
Exquisite views, folding and unfolding.
Farmland bordered by forested mountains,
across miles-wide flat valleys
towards the sea's edge,
approaching Dundee.

Scotland

BEN NEVIS

Gulls swarm down the railway platform
at Mallaig, west highland fishing port,
with boats well-used and brightly coloured.
Passing Morar,
the out-tide leaves patterns of seaweed
on shiny silt.
To Arisaig and Lochailort,
with four, five, six levels of peaks.
Steep, rounded and striped
with pine forests,
before snow-filled Glenfinnan.
Highland colours glow at early evening.
Shadows of mountains rush with the train
through Loch Eil to Benavie,
as we near Fort William
and softening hills,
until a shape in the distance
claims attention.
The powerful contours
of Ben Nevis.

Scotland

TOWARDS LOCH LOMOND

From Glasgow, north
through Helensburgh Upper.
Boat-filled bay lies below
vaulted, moulded mountains,
approaching Garelochead's
extraordinary highland views.
Wild pink foxgloves
contrast summer-green textures.
Passing Arrochar and Tarbet,
Ben Lomond overlooks
Loch Lomond's tree-rimmed islands
and fir-covered banks.
Beneath its bald peaks,
hills climb back through deep waters,
like steps into the distance.
Jagged, rugged summits
on either side of valley.
Loch surrounded and sheltered
to Ardlui,
where trains edge their way round
steep escarpment, forging upwards,
past heather patches, mosses
and pine forests,
to Crianlarich.

Scotland

WITTENHAM CLUMPS

From Oxford to Didcot.
Late summer, a July field's ripe grain
waiting to be taken up.
Some already harvested.
Straw-coloured heaps
on stubbled ground,
alongside patterns of sweeping green,
dark umber and golden tan.
Passing Appleford,
Wittenham Clumps in the distance.
Two hills, merging into one form.
Sparse trees on the left hill,
a broad copse on the other.
Strong, filled outlines on two mounds.
An iron-age hill fortress,
overseeing the flat farms
approaching Didcot.

DERBY TO MATLOCK

Derby, church spires
and open farmland, wide pastures,
passing through hillside villages
and red-brick chimneys.
To Duffield,
with its Georgian
and Victorian houses
and dark stone farm buildings
bordering the track.
The River Derwent,
filled with tall marsh-reeds,
passes through thick sloping forests,
deepest of green-grass valleys,
and bracken-covered stone
to Ambergate, Whatstandwill
and hillside towns and farms.
To Matlock Bath's sheer-faced escarpment –
cable cars leading to
the Heights of Abraham.
Deep tunnel opens
to views of Riber Castle,
high across the Derwent valley
from Matlock.

The Midlands

TOWARDS HEREFORD

Views over Port Meadow,
Oxford's city – wide open space,
common ground, grazing for horses
and cattle.
Through close trees to Handborough,
then deep earth, rich Oxfordshire
farming country to Charlbury,
with wide fields on soft slopes.
The soil changes hue from dark maroon
to russet.
Hedgerows are interspersed
with timber fences.
The feel of the land is different, special.
Moving through a broad valley to Kingham
with darkened earth tones,
pockets of ploughed ground
interwoven with bright green
and Cotswold stone farms,
yellow, grey, ochre,
lichen-covered old stone,
blending into the landscape,
naturally built, positioned,
to Moreton-in-Marsh.

The Midlands

BIRMINGHAM NEW STREET
TO WOLVERHAMPTON

Leaving Birmingham, the Telecom Tower
rises over the city dusk sky.
Rose colour over steel construction,
high-rise flats and church spires.
Brick terraces to Sandwell and Dudley.
Triangular, rectangular, cylindrical
structures.
Chimneys to industry,
mill buildings, some in use,
some with blackened windows,
awaiting development.
Sky has turned to water ripples,
grey mosaics with street-light reflections,
pink streaks above black high-rise silhouettes,
white picture windows, stark against
the deepening sky.
Sunset skeleton trees, images of a tropical
evening. Upon reaching Wolverhampton,
light confuses landscape; is it Jamaica
or a hot Caribbean distance?
Or to the right, industrial concrete pyramids
and warehouses.
Red street lights becoming yellow,
rectangular spheres.
Limpid canals, winding, not through
summer green willows,
but hundred-year-old brick enclosures.
Working buildings, purposeful structures.
The strengthened steel spine of Britain
holding the soft, lush countryside
to its timber bones.

The Midlands

116

TO BANBURY

Rapeseed jungles, late spring.
Wild, fluorescent yellow
penetrates the soft green country
between Oxford and Banbury.
Colour causing adjoining land
to take on exotic, equatorial hues
and be overtaken by magenta
wild flowers with turquoise leaves
in ultramarine hedges.

The Midlands

118

GORING AND
STREATLEY HILLS

Didcot to Reading,
January clouds and ploughed terrain.
Allotments, lakes, gardens
leading to orchards and pastures, with
corrugated iron roofs for straw shelter.
Roads cross the train line, passing
through flooded fields with
tractor tracks, highlighting shiny
white water on the rich, darkened earth.
Gulls descend, expecting seeds
as soon as they are planted, and
beige sheep stand quietly
in the mid-winter landscape.
Horses are blanketed, snow feels imminent,
trees bare their skeletal forms.
The Thames, with rust-grey reflections
passes through Goring and Streatley hills.
Copper beech trees, dark auburn,
create a contrast to winter-green.
Hills changing, multi-coloured,
always uncompromisingly beautiful;
preserved, subdued, shining
or caught in the midst of thunderous
storms, with fingerprint smudged clouds,
to Pangbourne and Reading.

The Midlands

120

Brenda Turner '85

THE RIDGEWAY

Ridgeway views,
from Didcot to Swindon.
Long vertical landscape.
Farms formed by ruled shapes.
Horizontal stripes of ice-green
and blue, interwoven with gold.
Building a deep texture,
layer on layer.
A carpet,
tantalizing to the touch,
of fabric woven by the plough,
and fastened by hedge trees.
Spreading, covering,
to the distant broad plateaux
of Berkshire and Gloucestershire.
Then leading through Chippenham
and the elegant Spa town, Roman waters
and yellow stone terraces of Bath,
to Bristol Port.

The Midlands

OXFORD CANAL

Oxford to Banbury to Leamington Spa.
Cold, mid-winter day, clear.
Spring just a month away.
Soft grasses and only a few days of snow,
but winter can come again, suddenly.
Vivid green fields, multi-shadowed
backdrop, cloud sky
with days lengthening.
Passing Cotswold stone villages
heading north.
Nearly-adult swans, almost pure white,
with only a few brown feathers
betraying their youth.
Thames level, like a bath filled
but not overflowing.
Idyllic day, sun hangs low in the sky.
Rows of canal boats, brightly painted,
slow-moving machines,
ready to emerge from winter's hibernation,
waiting for the warmth,
as well as the light, of the sun.
Travelling alongside the Oxford Canal,
sheep grazing, mounds of peat
and ploughed land approaching Banbury.
To Leamington Spa, terraced town.
The sun burns its mid-February way
into the carriage, bringing spring security.

LEAMINGTON SPA TO COVENTRY, SUNSET

May evenings lengthen into
thickening trees, with buds
swelling and filling skeleton frames.
Low slopes, smooth sheep pastures,
and specialized hills
riding on the distance,
to Leamington Spa.
Fields segmented, deep ochre,
beige and turquoise,
shimmering in the pale rose light
nearing Coventry.

The Midlands

The following pictures were lent with kind permission:

Towards Brighton	Patricia Wells
Towards Dover	Myra, John, Mathew and Joanna Cottingham
Norfolk Broads	Fitzwilliam College, Cambridge
Ersk Valley	Riga Forbes
Wittenham Clumps	Sheila, Peter and Anthony Glazebrook
Goring and Streatley Hills	Imogen, Sophie and Tom Smallwood
Ridgeway	Freya and Peter Holmes
Stirling to Dundee	Fitzwilliam College, Cambridge